Save Water

Kay Barnham

WAYLAND

First published in Great Britain in 2006 by
Wayland, an imprint of Hachette Children's Books

Hachette Children's Books
338 Euston Road, London NW1 3BH

Editor: Penny Worms
Senior Design Manager: Rosamund Saunders
Designer: Ben Ruocco, Tall Tree Ltd

British Library Cataloguing in Publication Data
Barnham, Kay
        Saving water. – (Environment action)
        1. Water conservation – Juvenile literature
        I. Title
        333.9'116

ISBN 10: 0 7502 4866 1
ISBN 13: 978 0 7502 4866 2

Printed in China

The publishers would like to thank the following for allowing us to
reproduce their pictures in this book:
Alamy: 14 (Ethel Davies), 20 (mediacolour's), 25
(plainpicture/Usbeck.P), 29 (John Walmsley). Corbis images: 7 (Geray
Sweeney), 18 (Kontos Yannis), 22 (Edward Bock), 26 (Johnny Buzzerio).
Ecoscene: 5 (NASA), 15 (Angela Hampton), 16 (Rosemary Greenwood), 17
(Paul Ferraby), 24 (Angela Hampton), 28 (Stephen Coyne). Getty
images: 4 (Peter Essick), 13 (Gavin Hellier), 23 (Kroeger/Gross). Rex
Features: 10 (Sipa Press). Photolibrary: cover and 27 (Peter Fogg).
Wayland Picture Library: title page and 12, 6, 8, 9, 11, 19, 21.

Contents

All About Water

Water has no taste, no smell and no colour. At first glance, you might think that it is quite dull. But it is actually very important. Without water, we could not survive.

△ More than half of your body is made of water. Every day, the water you lose must be replaced by more water.

Luckily, much of the earth's **surface** is covered in water. It is found in seas, lakes, rivers and streams. Ice and snow are made of frozen water.

△ This is what our planet looks like from space. The green and brown is land. The blue is water. The white is clouds and ice. There's an awful lot of water here!

5

The Water Cycle

The amount of water on our planet never changes. No more water appears. No water vanishes. Instead, water moves from place to place. The water that you drink might once have tumbled down a **waterfall** on the other side of the world.

△ Water moves in lots of different ways. This water will eventually reach the sea.

The **water cycle** describes the way water moves around, over and over again.

- The sun warms the sea causing **water vapour** to rise into the air.
- As it rises and cools, it turns into tiny **droplets** of water.
- The droplets of water form clouds.
- Wind blows the clouds over land.
- When the droplets of water in the clouds become too big and heavy, they fall as rain.
- Water flows down streams and rivers until it reaches the sea again.

▽ As these clouds are blown towards the higher ground, rain will fall.

Why Save Water?

If there is so much water in the world, why do we need to save it? The answer is simple – only a small amount of the water can be used. It is important that we look after this water carefully.

△ The salty water in the sea cannot be used for drinking or washing. Drinking lots of sea water could make you very ill.

△ More people means more water is needed.

There is another problem. The world's population is growing bigger every year, but there is no extra water. By using less water, we can make sure that there is enough to go round.

FACT!

In 1980, the world's population was 4,450 million. By 2005, there were another 2,000 million people living on our planet!

A Cleaner World

Pollution is dirty or unhealthy air or water. It can cause huge problems around the world, harming people, animals and plants. Many people are concerned about pollution and do their best to stop it. They want the world to be a cleaner, healthier place.

△ When **chemicals** from **factories** and **sewers** pour into rivers and streams, the water becomes polluted.

The dirty smoke that comes from factory chimneys does not just pollute the air. Clouds carry the pollution to different places, dropping polluted rain elsewhere. This **acid rain** can **destroy** forests.

△ When oil tankers spill their load into the sea, this causes terrible harm to coastlines and wildlife. It takes a lot of effort to clean it up.

Surface Water

Most of the water we use comes from the earth's surface. Fresh water flows along rivers and streams, and is stored in lakes. It is cleaned and then **piped** to homes, offices, factories and farms.

◁ Water is pumped from rivers like this to wherever it is needed.

A **dam** is a strong wall built across a river **valley**. Instead of flowing to the sea, the water is trapped behind the dam. This water can be used when the weather is dry and water supplies are low.

△ The water held back by a dam is called a **reservoir**. Just like natural lakes, reservoirs are home to wildlife.

Groundwater

Some of the water we use does not come from rivers, streams or dams. When water soaks into the ground, it is hidden below the surface in gaps between layers of rock. This is known as **groundwater**.

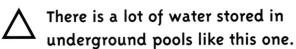 There is a lot of water stored in underground pools like this one.

It costs more to use groundwater than surface water. This is because it is harder to reach than a river or reservoir. First, a hole is dug down to the level of the water. Then the water is pumped to the surface.

A **well** is a deep hole that reaches down to the water underground. Water is brought up to the surface by a bucket.

Waste Water

When water is washed down the sink or **flushed** down the toilet, it cannot be poured straight back into a river or the sea. It is far too dirty. Instead, it travels down pipes to a **wastewater treatment works**, where it will be cleaned.

△ The place where toilet water is cleaned is called a **sewage plant**.

After being treated, the water is now clean enough to be pumped back into rivers and the sea.

At the wastewater treatment works, the water is cleaned. It runs through **coarse** layers of stones, then finer ones of sand, to remove waste. Any remaining **germs** are killed by a special type of light or by chemicals.

FACT!

If waste water were not treated, it would cause dreadful harm to wildlife and the **environment**.

Sea Water

Sea water is very salty. It cannot be used for drinking, cooking, washing or for watering crops. People living on small islands and in hot, dry countries may be surrounded by sea water but have very little fresh water. Here, they have a special way of removing salt from sea water. Then the water can be used as normal.

△ **Submarines** also get the fresh water they use on board by removing salt from sea water.

When water vapour rises from the sea to form clouds, the salt is left behind in the sea. So rain is always fresh water.

△ The next time it rains, imagine where the water might have come from. Maybe it was from the Pacific or Atlantic Oceans!

Turn It Off!

The easiest way to save water is by turning the tap off. Millions of litres of clean, fresh water disappear down plugholes every day. Before it can be used again, it must be pumped away, cleaned and then pumped back. Turning taps off saves water and energy!

△ If you leave the tap running while you brush your teeth, you could use as much as six litres of water.

Did you know that the drips taken from one tap during one week would be enough to fill a bath with water? So it's important to make sure a tap is turned off completely.

△ In some countries, people are not lucky enough to have fresh water piped to their homes. Instead, they have to carry water long distances in buckets.

Saving Water at Home

There are lots of ways that you can save water at home. Have a quick shower instead of a bath. You'll still be clean, but you'll save water!

◁ Make sure the washing machine or dishwasher is full before running it. That way you won't use it so many times.

If you pour yourself a drink of water, don't run the tap to make sure the water is really cold. Add ice cubes to your glass or cool a jug of water in the fridge instead.

The small tank above a toilet is called a **cistern**. It is filled with water, which rushes down the toilet when you **flush**. By putting a special bag into the toilet cistern, there is room for less water. This means that less water is used each time the toilet is flushed.

FACT!

In the UK, each person uses enough water to fill 16 buckets every single day!

Saving Water in the Garden

Some people use huge amounts of water to keep their gardens green and healthy. By leaving a **water butt** or a bucket outside, you can collect rainwater when the weather is wet and use the water when the weather is dry.

◁ A water sprinkler can use as much water in one hour as a family of four uses in a whole day! A watering can uses much less water.

When it rains, put houseplants outdoors to soak up the shower. Then you won't need to water them so often.

△ If you like to grow plants, pick those that don't need much water. A **cactus** needs hardly any!

Saving Water at School

At school, each pupil uses up to 4,000 litres of water a year – that's enough to fill a bath every week! There are lots of ways schools and pupils can reduce this amount.

Report any leaky pipes that you see. Water companies can come to check that there are no leaks in the school or in the pipes underground.

A **water meter** measures how much water is being used. Ask to check your school's meter. Then you'll be able to see how much water you're saving!

△ Put a plug in a sink before turning the tap on to wash your hands so you don't use more water than needed. When you've finished, make sure you turn taps off properly.

More Ideas!

Rainwater harvesting is a way of collecting water. As rain falls on roofs, it pours into water butts or tanks underground. The rainwater can then be used for flushing the toilet, washing clothes and watering the garden.

△ Water that runs off the roofs of these huts in Belize is being collected in a water butt.

Place a small washing-up bowl into a large sink. That way, you'll use less water when you wash up. If you're boiling a kettle, only pour in as much water as you need. You'll use less water and the kettle will take less time to boil.

△ By using a bucket of water and a sponge to wash a car, instead of a hose pipe, you'll save litres of water.

Glossary

Acid rain – polluted water that falls as rain

Cactus – a plant covered in prickles that grows in hot, dry places

Chemicals – powerful liquids or powders that can be used for lots of things, including cleaning

Cistern – a small tank of water above a toilet

Coarse – made of large, rough pieces

Dam – a strong wall built across a river valley to hold back water

Destroy – to break or damage something so that it is beyond repair

Droplet – a tiny amount of liquid

Environment – everything around us which affects how we live

Factories – buildings where people make things with machines

Flushed – washed away with water

Germs – tiny living things that sometimes cause disease

Groundwater – water that is found underground

Piped – when a liquid or gas is sent down a tube

Pollution – dirty or unhealthy air or water

Population – the number of people who live in a country or place

Reservoir – a man-made lake

Sewage plant – a place where dirty toilet water is cleaned

Sewers – pipes that take away dirty toilet water to a sewage plant

Submarine – a ship that can travel underwater

Surface – the outside or top of something

Valley – a deep dip in the land, usually containing a flowing river

Wastewater treatment works – a place where dirty water is cleaned

Water butt – a large barrel that catches rainwater

Water cycle – how water moves around the world

Waterfall – a stream or river of water falling from a high place to a low place

Water vapour – tiny droplets of water in the air

Well – a hole dug to get water out of the ground

Index